The World of Print

by Wendy Body and Stan Cullimore

Contents

Section 1

Section 2

Section 3

Edinburgh Gate
Harlow, Essex

Conversation between Two Authors:
Wendy Body and Stan Cullimore

Have you ever tried having a written conversation? We did!

Wendy I'll start! I know you were a pop star with The Housemartins before you became writer, but what actually started you off as an author?

Stan The first stories I wrote were for my son. I used to tell him that his toy hippo came to life when he was asleep. When he was in bed, I would tell him the stories that the hippo "told" me. These stories were later published as the series of *Henrietta* books.

Wendy OK, but why did you give up being a pop star?

Stan It just stopped being the thing I wanted to do. Instead of writing songs, I wanted to write stories. I always said that my favourite bit of playing concerts was talking to the audience in between songs.

Wendy Did they answer back?!

Stan Yes! They used to shout and tell me to get on with the singing! Anyway, what about you? How did you get into writing?

Wendy I've always written stories since I was a little girl and when I was working as a teacher I decided that I'd try and get something published. I thought it might earn me more money than teaching! I found out that most children's writers don't get paid a lot of money, but I did eventually earn enough to give up teaching and become a full-time writer. It's a great life and I really enjoy writing, don't you?

Stan Of course! I love it! But what do you think is the hardest bit?

Wendy Ummmm … sitting in front of a blank screen when you can't think what to write and you've got a deadline to meet … revising the same piece of writing over and over to get something you're really satisfied with. What about you? What do you think is the hardest part?

Stan I'm not sure. Could you pour me another cup of coffee while I think about it?

Wendy All right – as long as you get the next one!

Wendy: I'll start! I know you were a pop star with The Housemartins before you became a writer, but what actually started you off as an author?
Stan: The first stories I wrote were for my son. I used to tell him that his toy hippo came to life when he was asleep. When he was in bed, I would tell him stories that the hippo "told" me. These stories were later published as the series of Henrietta books.
Wendy: OK, but why did you give up being a pop star?
Stan: It just stopped being the thing I wanted to do. Instead of writing songs, I wanted to

➡A page of conversation from the author's notebook

Stan OK. I agree with you about writing: the hardest part is worrying about running out of things to write – running out of ideas.

Wendy Children always ask me what I do if I get stuck for ideas – what do you do if it happens to you?

Stan I either take my dog (a little Jack Russell called Meg) out for a walk or I go for a swim. Both things help me to think.

Wendy I'm a bit like that – I walk round the garden or go out with the dogs (two Yorkshire terriers called Merlin and Muffin). Most of the time though, I don't have too much trouble in thinking what to write – I suppose writing is a kind of habit that you get into. It does help to bounce ideas off other people though, doesn't it?

Stan Yes – like when we wrote the *Mai Ling* books together. Do you remember that?

Wendy How could I forget? It cost me a fortune in chocolate biscuits every time you came round!

Stan You ate just as many as me!

Wendy Rubbish! I had two at the most! Anyway, get on with answering the question!

Stan It was fun writing those books … I remember that when one of us had a good idea (or a bad one) the other one would burst out laughing! We wrote them quite quickly, really.

Wendy I wanted you to hurry up because I've just thought of two good questions for you …

1 Which book are you most proud of?

2 Aaaah! Writing that has made me forget the other one!

Stan I've been asked that question quite a few times …

Wendy Give me the notebook – I've remembered the other question! What else do you write apart from children's books?

Stan Hang on, I haven't answered the first question yet. I always think that the book I'm most proud of is the one I've just finished writing. Which of your books is your favourite?

Wendy That's a hard question … I'm really not sure. I think because writers create things, you're usually proud of what you've created – especially if someone thinks it's good enough to publish …

Stan So how many books have you written?

Wendy No, let me go back to the other question. I think the book I'm most proud of is not one that I actually wrote but one that I compiled. I put together poems, extracts from other writers' stories (and a little bit of my own writing) and made an anthology called *A World War II Anthology*. One reason I'm proud of it is because it's dedicated to my uncle who was killed in World War II before I was born. To answer your other question, I've written over a hundred books for children, teachers and parents. Now YOU answer MY other question!

Stan Which one? You ask so many!

Wendy I'm nosy! The one about: do you only write children's books?

Stan No. I spend a lot of time writing television scripts for children's animated programmes.

Wendy Which do you most like doing?

Stan Both! It's like trying to decide which is best – chocolate or ice-cream. Whenever I get too much of one thing, I do the other – if that makes sense!

Wendy Which is hardest, writing a script or writing a book?

Stan Neither. In fact, they are both the same thing, really. You're just telling a story. The only difference is that with a script I have to put in quite a few technical words – telling the director how to film each scene.

Wendy OK, enough of that. Here's a good one … how would you describe yourself?

Stan Charming, handsome, rich, kind …

Wendy … and not very truthful!

Stan WHAT?! Anyway, how would you describe yourself?

Wendy MORE charming, etc. etc!! Let's be serious … how would you describe your normal working day?

Stan Very long, very hard work, sometimes frustrating, sometimes brilliant.

Wendy Me too. Let's stop now … Where's that cup of coffee you were going to get me?

Stan Chocolate biscuit?

Newspaper Reporter: *Myra Lee*

? What is your job title?

A Senior reporter.

? How long have you worked for the *Bristol Evening Post*?

A I joined the *Evening Post* as a senior reporter a year ago.

? Was that your first job?

A No. I started work in July 1992 after graduating from Birmingham University. My first job was a junior reporter with a weekly paper in the Midlands. After two years I joined an evening paper, similar to the *Evening Post*, in Coventry. I was there for three years. Then I worked as a reporter and producer for Live TV in Birmingham.

Newspaper reporter Myra Lee (right)

? What qualifications did you need for your job?

A A good all-round education is essential for all reporters. But English and spelling are really important. Often reporters have been to university. But all reporters do a course in journalism. Sometimes they do this before starting the job, other times it is on-the-job training.

I did a six-month course in journalism at Hastings. This taught me about writing and interviewing skills, law, shorthand, local government knowledge and typing. Since then, I have done a number of computer courses related to newspapers.

BT West of England Newspaper of the Year

EVENING POST

THE PAPER AT THE HEART OF BRISTOL

30p

BRISTOL

No. 20,703

Monday, April 24, 2000

mic books are Go!
ival of heroes hits town
–Page 12

We need to get nasty
says City skipper Keith Millen
–See Back Page

TWO CINEMA TICKETS FOR THE PRICE OF ONE — SEE PAGE 14

en shares £1,000 snack windfall with neighbour

INSIDE TONIGHT

Family in fire drama

KINGSWOOD: A family of six had a lucky escape after a fire broke out at their home as they slept.
● Full story: Page 2

Soccer thugs

FISHPONDS: A pub was wrecked during fighting by thugs after the Bristol Rovers v Bristol City soccer derby.
● Full story: Page 3

Car cruisers

WESTON-super-MARE: Up to 500 youths gathered for an illegal car cruise.
● Full story: Page 5

What job did you want to do when you were a child?
I always wanted to be a reporter from as early as I can remember.

What part of your job do you enjoy the most?
I enjoy meeting different people and learning something about them. No two days are alike in journalism. One day you might be interviewing an old lady who has lost her cat, the next you might be meeting the Prime Minister.

What part do you enjoy least?
Sometimes as a journalist you have to spend many hours at your desk in front of your computer writing lots and lots of stories. It can be very tiring.

Do many of your friends work in similar jobs?
Yes, nearly all of them. As a journalist you often work long unsociable hours and therefore you tend to socialise with other journalists.

What do you like to do when you are not working?
My family live a long way from Bristol and I often use my time off to visit them. I also play netball.

Were you keen on writing as a child?
My favourite subject at school was English – particularly writing. (I was also good at R.E. and I enjoyed that too.) I loved writing. I would often write stories for my little sister and read them to her at bedtime.

Do you think you will always work in newspaper publishing?
I hope so, but things are changing all the time. I have already done some television journalism and I am currently working with Bristol's "107.3 FM – The Eagle" radio at weekends.

The newsroom at the Bristol Evening Post

? What kind of qualities do you think you need to have to be a successful reporter?

A You need to be able to mix with people in any situation, ask lots of questions to find out about them and most importantly listen to what they say. At school you should work hard, particularly at English, and think creatively.

? Do you have your own office or desk area? What is it like?

A I have my own desk, but it is in a group of desks with eight others. We make up a kind of team in the newsroom which is a big office with lots of journalists. We all have to work together in newspapers to make sure we get the paper out, so it is important we are all in the same room.

? Are all your working days the same?

A No two days are the same for a journalist. I start work usually at 7.30 a.m. My boss is the news editor and he will come and tell me what stories he wants me to work on that day. You cannot predict what may happen from one day to the next. He may ring me at home or on my mobile and say, "Go to such and such, Myra, there's a big fire or an accident."

First thing in the morning we always ring the police, fire brigade and ambulance service to see what has been happening in the night. Then we ring them each hour to keep a check on things. Other regular jobs for reporters involve covering court cases, council meetings and other sorts of meetings our readers might be interested in.

? What do you think have been the main changes in newspaper publishing over the past 20 years?

A Computers have made things very different in the newspaper world. We can now create a newspaper on a computer.

Technology has also helped us to gather information. We can now write stories from home using e-mail to send them to work or even dictate them down a mobile phone. But technology has also had a negative effect on newspapers in recent years. There are many other ways available for people to get news and sales of newspapers have dropped.

? What advice would you give to someone who wanted to be a reporter when they left school?

A
1. Work hard at school – especially in English.
2. Try to be a good speller!
3. Learn how to talk to a wide variety of people and listen to what they have to say.
4. Learn to drive a car when you are old enough so you can dash off when a big story breaks.

? What is the most Interesting story you have worked on?

A When I worked on the *Coventry Evening Telegraph*, photographer Barbara Evripidou and I covered the war in Bosnia. We flew out with the army twice. It was very scary at times and very cold. The hours were long and tiring, but the things we saw will stay in our minds forever. It was also good to know that what we were reporting was telling people back home about a war a thousand miles away.

Another interesting story was when I was working in television. I was responsible for covering a big political meeting with all the world leaders (Tony Blair, President Bill Clinton and many others). It was very exciting meeting them all.

Newspaper Photographer: *Barbara Evripidou*

? How long have you worked for the *Bristol Evening Post* as a newspaper photographer?

A I have been here about a year and a half.

? Was this your first job? If not, what did you do before?

A I worked in different parts of the country on regional newspapers and agencies for six years.

? What experience did you need for your present job?

A Working in different newspapers and experience with news, sport and community photography.

? Did you receive any special training to do your present job?

A Yes, I took a special course in Sheffield – the National Council for the Training of Journalists press photography diploma.

? What job did you want to do when you were at school?

A I wanted a job that meant I didn't have to sit in an office all day, a job that would offer me variety.

? Which parts of your job do you enjoy the most and the least?

A I really enjoy going through the day's work and finding a photo I really like from the ones that I've taken. What I don't like is having to stand out in the rain or when it's really cold to take a picture.

? What do you like to do when you are not working?

A I live in Bristol and I like going on long walks around the city and exploring on foot. It makes such a difference to get out of the car and leave the mobile phone at home.

? What was your favourite subject when you were at school?

A Definitely art and English. I really liked painting and making things. I still read a lot (well, whenever I can) and that comes from liking reading at school.

? When did your interest in photography start?

A I did a BTEC in Art and Design when I was 17. Photography was just a small part of the course, but it was the first time I'd used a "real" camera, so it all stems from there.

? Do you think you will always work in newspapers?

A I'd like to think I'll always work in newspapers, although the thought of travelling the world and taking pictures does appeal to me.

? What kind of qualities do you think you need to be a successful photographer?

A You need the technical skills and ability, of course, but you also need the ability to adapt easily, depending on the circumstances, because news changes all the time. Most important of all, you need to be able to get on with people instantly.

Barbara took this photo for the Bristol Evening Post

? Do you have your own office or desk area? What is it like?

A The photographers share an office which has two film-processing machines, four computers, a studio and a "den" where we have our own filing cabinets and somewhere to catch up on the day's events.

? Are your working days always the same?

A No, each day is completely different. One day you could be photographing the Lord Mayor presenting a cheque, the next day you could be in a helicopter photographing an incident from the skies.

? Can you tell us a bit about the cameras you use? Do you use a digital camera? Roughly how many films do you use a week?

A We will be using digital cameras very soon. At present, we use film cameras, and I have three of those, plus various lenses which enable me to photograph all kinds of scenarios. I use about 30–40 rolls of film a week. Each film contains 36 exposures.

? How many shots would you take for each published photo? Which kinds of shot are the most difficult to take?

A It depends. On average, I use about a roll of film for each job, but football would probably need about seven rolls, and a feature would need about three. Animal pictures can be the most difficult to take. You try telling a three-month-old puppy to sit still!

? Do you develop your own films?

A No, we have film-processing machines to develop the film. There are technicians that work in the department to help us scan in our images.

? What do you think have been the main changes in newspaper photography over the past 20 years?

A The change from black and white to colour … the speed of things – motor drives and now digital cameras.

Barbara took this photo of an event from the BBC's Music Live festival for the Bristol Evening Post

BBC
Music Live
25-29 May 2000

? What advice would you give to someone who wanted to be a professional photographer when they left school?

A Pick up a camera as soon as you can and experiment. Photograph what interests you and find new ways of showing that image. Try doing some work experience at your local newspaper to find out what it's all about. Every photographer finds their own way in if they really want it.

? What is the most interesting assignment you have worked on? What is the worst?!

A The most interesting was when I was invited to go to Bosnia with the army just after the war was over – to see the rebuilding programmes. It was an eye-opener for me to see the extent of the devastation. It was also interesting to see how the army works in these circumstances.

This is the worst! I was going on a job to photograph a newly sponsored youth football team. I wasn't wearing my usual jacket. I took the photographs, thanked everyone, got back to the office and, to my horror, I couldn't find the film. So I rang everyone up and begged them to go back so I could take their photographs again. They weren't too happy, but they all agreed to do it. I quickly snapped some pics and let them go on their way.

Then … when I got back to the office, I found the original film in my jacket! How embarrassing!

Illustrator:
Philippe Dupasquier

? Did you always want to be an illustrator?

A I always enjoyed drawing since I was a little boy and it came almost naturally that I ended up in an art school. (I was good at nothing else according to my teachers!) I dreamed of becoming a comic-strip illustrator, but at the end of my training, I also wanted to be a painter. In the end, I became an illustrator and because I had a few ideas for stories, I started to write as well.

Philippe Dupasquier drew this picture of himself

? Do you find any problems with that?

A I find the writing difficult. Being French and living in England, I can mix the two languages together, which can be a bit of a mess! I also have the bad habit of believing that sometimes using pictures only is enough to tell a story (it is actually!) and it makes me a bit lazy about writing.

? You said you wanted to be a comic-strip illustrator; did you read a lot of comics as a boy?

A Yes, and my favourite books were the *Tintin* stories. We had the whole collection in my family. I particularly liked these books because they were full of different characters having adventures all over the world. I still read a lot of European comics which I bring back from France when I go there on holiday.

? What do you do if you get stuck for ideas?

A First, I try not to panic and keep very cool about it, as everybody knows that being stressed over a problem is not going to resolve it. Then I realise that doesn't work and I get completely stressed and depressed. Soon I reach the deep end and start thinking about looking for a new job. But suddenly, a small idea creeps in and it starts to grow and grow until it becomes a new book and once again you feel you are at the top of the world.

? What is your favourite medium to work in?

A I like working in watercolours because it is spontaneous and fast which goes well with my natural style of drawing and painting.

? Do you have a special routine when you are working?

A If I am hooked on an idea or a project, I get up early and I work until I am just too tired to carry on – usually at the end of the day. If I'm not hooked on anything in particular, I can spend a nice day in the library looking at books or a day out on my bike sketching things outdoors. Sometimes I do the shopping and the washing and the hoovering and the ironing and go to bed exhausted, hoping that I will find inspiration the next day.

Q Is there any book that you are particularly proud of? Anything you find particularly exciting?

A I try not to look back at what I have done in the past because it can be quite distracting to what you are currently working on or to some future project. Generally, the very thing that you are working on at the moment is the only thing that counts – the rest feels like it's done, finished, consumed.

Succeeding is exciting. I don't necessarily mean having a whole book being successful. It can be just a small success, like discovering how to draw a certain thing – such as a train going fast. Drawing is a lot to do with understanding how things work. Often you spend a lot of time wondering, until one day you just find out and that is very rewarding.

? Do you use your artistic talents for anything apart from drawing or painting?

A I love making paper models like boats, planes, birds, animals, etc. They usually stay for a while on my windowsill or shelves, until they get dusty and not so attractive after all. Then they end up in the bin, after which a new one comes along. I also like collecting small objects which I find visually attractive. It can be a plastic toy, or a funny shaped sponge … anything.

? Here's a difficult question … How would you describe yourself?

A On certain days I'm charming, talented, brilliant, strong and fearless. But on some other days I'm absolutely the complete opposite! In other words, sometimes I'm confident, sometimes I'm not.

? Do you have any advice for someone who wants to be an illustrator?

A Whatever you do, whatever you think, however bad things can be sometimes, don't give up. There is always light at the end of the tunnel – that is, if you don't get run over by the train first of course!

Book Publisher:
Catherine Allison

Publisher Catherine Allison talks to her editor about a new book

? What is your present job?

A My present job is Longman's Publisher for Primary School Literacy – I am the publisher for the books in the series you are reading right now! I started this job in the summer of 1999. Before that I was an editor and I worked on a range of school books – from history for 11-year-olds to design and technology for A Level students.

? How did you become a publisher?

A I left university with a degree in English and I really didn't know what I wanted to do … except that I wanted to work with books in some way. I also liked art – drawing and making things – so a job involving all of this seemed ideal. I had a number of different jobs. One of them was working in the book binding department of the university library cleaning and repairing books which were 400 years old. I loved that!

Gradually, I realised that publishing was what I wanted to do. It is such a popular area to work in that I knew I would need some more technical skills and business experience to "get in".

? How did you go about that?

A I took a diploma in publishing which gave me the basic editing skills and some experience of marketing and finance as well as printing, photography and graphic design. I really enjoyed the course so I was convinced that publishing was the right job for me.

? What was your first job?

A It was on a weekly magazine. The team was very small, so everyone had to do a bit of everything which I liked because it meant I learnt very quickly. Then in 1993 I moved to Longman's school book publishing as an editor, a job which I had for about six years.

Longman's Schools Division is a big organisation. Instead of doing a bit of everything, people specialise in editing, commissioning (finding authors) or production (organising the printing of books).

? What does an editor do, exactly?

A As an editor, I took a manuscript from an author and either edited it myself or found a freelance (self-employed) editor to do it. I then decided the size and style of the text and illustrations and wrote an artwork brief for the pictures. I worked with a graphic designer, illustrators and photographers to make the book look as attractive and helpful to the reader as possible. I would also talk to the author from time to time to make sure that he or she would be happy with the final result.

I had to make sure that the design, illustrations and photography were all ready on time and matched the budget – the amount of money which it will cost to publish a book. (The book budget covers everything, including payments to the author and illustrator, the cost of paper and printing.) Finally, the designed book is handed on to be printed and published.

All these stages are called the publishing process and it can take eight months or more to produce a book. I worked on anything from two to 42 books at a time (some had fewer pages than others!). Each one was at a different stage in the publishing process, so I was generally kept quite busy!

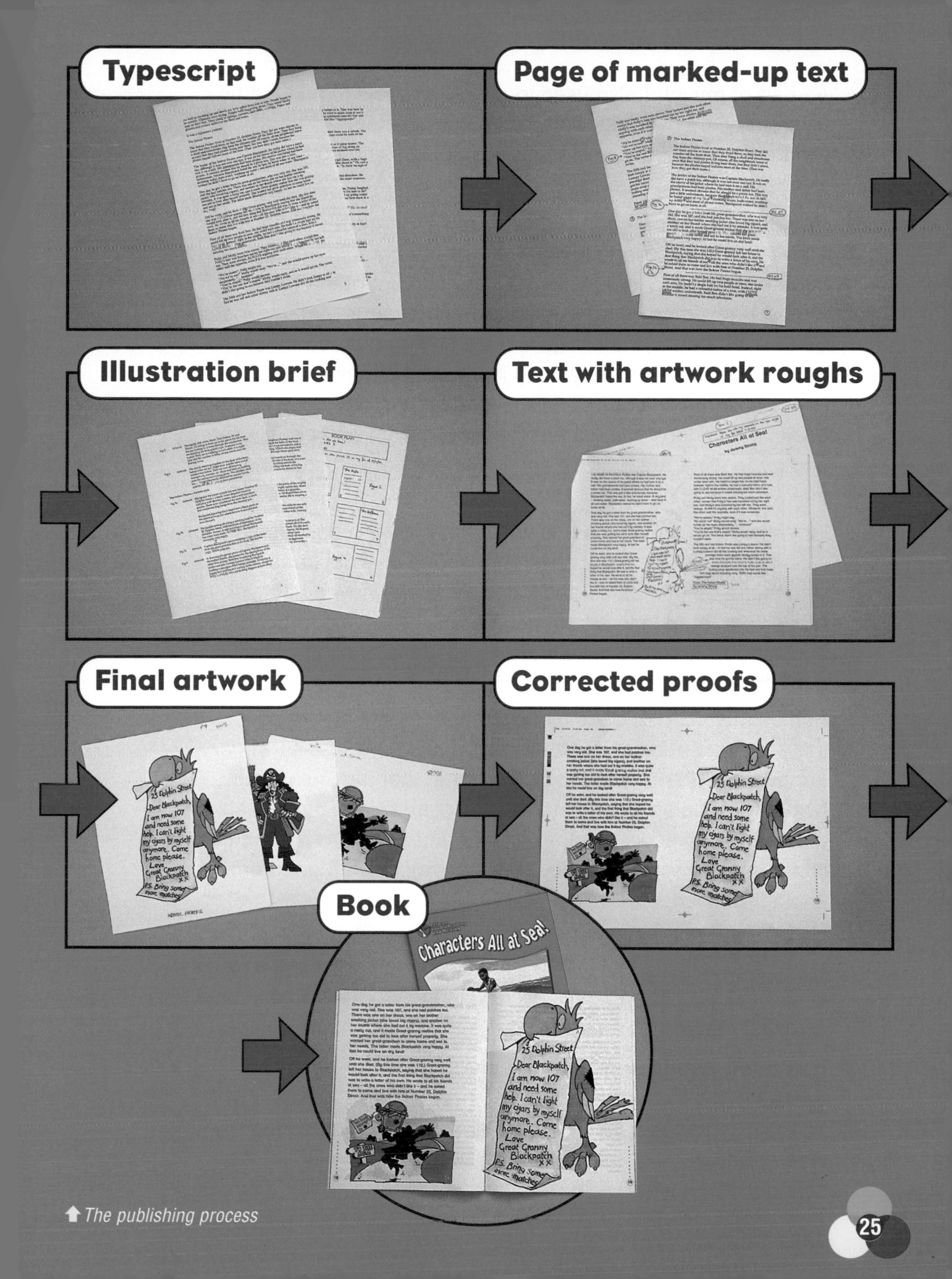

The publishing process

As part of my job I also used to go into schools to find out how different types of books were being used by teachers and children and to look at what other big publishing companies were publishing.

? How has your job changed now that you are a publisher?

A I am responsible for deciding what type of book or series to publish next. I have to think about the content of the book, forecast how many copies it will sell and over how many years. So I travel around the UK quite a lot, finding out about how teachers teach, what they need in the way of new books, what books children like or find difficult and testing out ideas for new books. I also look very carefully at books from other publishers and try to work out how we can make our books better than theirs!

I then have to find authors to write books on the right subject for a particular age group of children. I phone or write to authors who might be interested and I also try to find new authors. I receive a lot of letters from people who are trying to get their books published, but quite often these ideas don't fit with our publishing plans.

Sometimes schools have money to spend only at one point in the year, so I need to know this and make sure that new books are published and ready to be bought at that particular time. I work with the sales and marketing departments to make sure that teachers know about new books and to see how Longman can persuade schools to buy our book rather than one from another publisher.

It's very exciting to come up with a new idea for a book or series and to think that in a few months' time it will be in schools all around the UK and that children and teachers will be enjoying reading it.

? Has book publishing changed much over the past few years?

A Yes, publishing is a fast-moving industry, and even during my time at Longman, the way in which books are produced has changed so much. For instance, when I started in 1993, most authors sent in their manuscripts on paper, having typed them on manual or electric typewriters. Now nearly all authors use computers and send their manuscripts on disk or by e-mail. All the designers now use computers to design the pages, whereas in 1993, some designers still produced long strips of text called galleys which were cut up by hand and stuck on to page-layout grids. It seems very old-fashioned now and I'm sure that in another seven years the way we produce books will have changed again. Publishing books on CD-ROM and online is becoming more and more popular. One day soon you will be able to read books on televisions and mobile phones as well as on computer monitors. I'm looking forward to it!

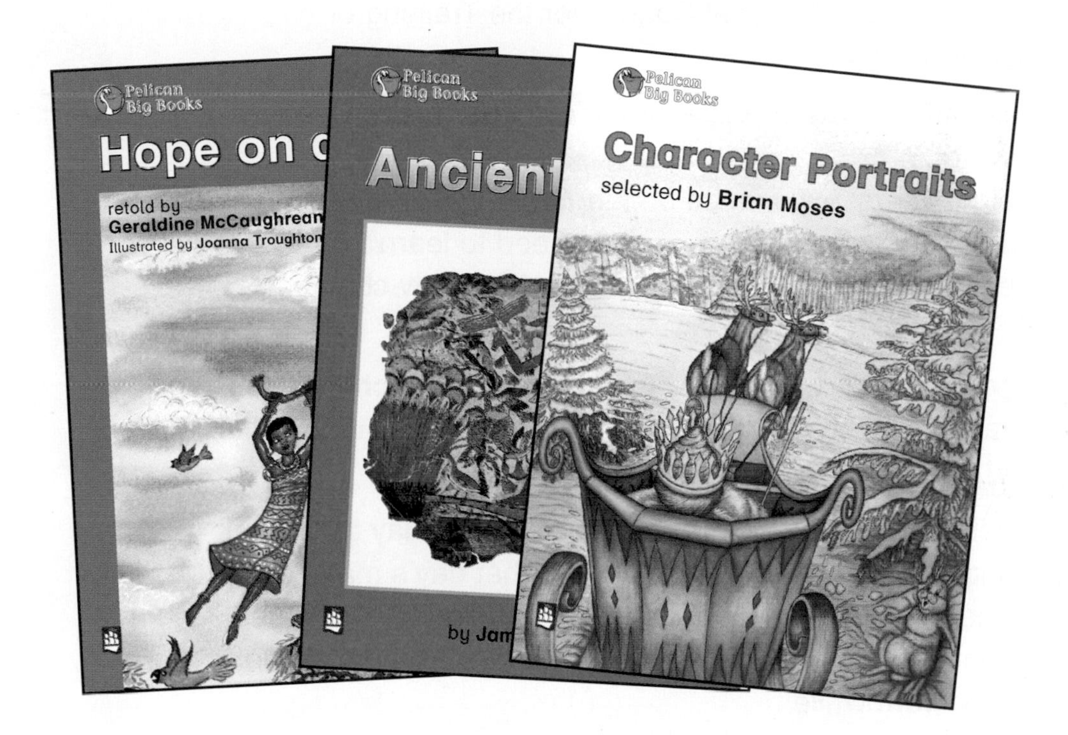

Some of the books that Catherine worked on when she was an editor.

Newspaper Sports Editor:
Chris Bartlett

? How long have you worked for the *Bristol Evening Post*?

A 18 years. When I first joined, I was a sports sub-editor involved in preparing copy – that's the stories and reports – for the newspaper. I also wrote headlines for the stories and reported on local football matches.

? Was that your first job? If not, what did you do before?

A I was a trainee journalist, writing news, sport and features material for various weekly newspapers in Devon and Cornwall. After three years as a trainee, I obtained my proficiency certificate from the National Council for the Training of Journalists.

? What qualifications or experience did you need for your present job?

A I had eight years' experience on the *Evening Post* sports desk, learning every aspect of the job. You need to learn to "think on your feet" and be ready to react quickly to rapidly changing situations.

? What job did you want to do when you were a child?

A Like many small boys, I wanted to be a professional footballer.

? What part of your job do you enjoy most?

A We publish a 48-page sports paper every Saturday afternoon, which includes reports and results from that day's matches. When the deadline for printing approaches and all the pages are completed on time, it's a great feeling and makes all the hard work worthwhile.

? What part do you enjoy least?

A Having to fill a lot of pages when most of the sport is cancelled because of bad weather.

? Do many of your friends work in similar jobs?

A Yes. People I worked with on my training course now work in national and regional media all over the country.

What do you like to do when you are not working?

Play golf, walk, cycle, listen to music, read biographies – so I can find out about other people's lives and jobs!

What's your favourite sport?

Football. It really is the game of the people. So many people of all ages watch the game and play it. Even the Queen goes to the FA Cup final sometimes.

Were you keen on sport as a child?

Yes, I played football, tennis and cricket. I broke my collarbone twice playing football in the street – but it didn't put me off.

Do you think you will always work in publishing newspapers or would you like to do something different?

I'm very happy working in sports journalism. If I had to switch careers, I would like to try being a golf caddy – that's someone who carries the bag of a professional golfer.

Chris Bartlett at his desk

? What kind of qualities do you think you need to be a successful sports editor?

A Most of all you need a real passion for all aspects of sport. You need to be bold enough to make the decisions which will determine the content and image of your newspaper.

? Do you have your own office? What is it like?

A No. I work in a big open-plan office alongside all the other journalists who work for the *Evening Post*.

? How many people work for you?

A There are 12 sports journalists (including me) who write the stories and design the pages. There is also a secretary who does a lot of the organisation and administration required to keep the department working efficiently.

? Can you describe a normal working day?

A I arrive at the office between 6 and 6.30 a.m. to prepare for the editor's conference at 7 a.m. He needs to know all about the content of the sports pages – what will be the main story on the back page, for example.

After the conference we work towards the deadline for the first edition, which is 9 a.m., then constantly make changes for each edition until our final deadline at 1.30 p.m. The stories we have will be updated and new ones will be happening – so there's always something going on.

We then start planning for the next day's newspaper, deciding which stories we are going to use and how we will present them. There's another editor's conference at 3.30 p.m.
The days are always different – there's always something new happening in the world of sport.

? What do you think have been the main changes in newspaper publishing over the past 20 years?

A
1. The switch from the old-fashioned, "hot metal" method of production to a modern system using word processors and computers.
2. Digital cameras are now used to scan photographic images directly into the computer.